An Almost Perfect Person

A COMEDY IN TWO ACTS

By Judith Ross

SAMUEL FRENCH, INC.

25 WEST 45TH STREET   NEW YORK 10036
7623 SUNSET BOULEVARD   HOLLYWOOD 90046
LONDON   *TORONTO*

AN ALMOST PERFECT PERSON was first presented by Burry Fredrik and Joel Key Rice at the Belasco Theatre, New York City, on October 27, 1977. It was directed by Zoe Caldwell, the scenery and lighting were designed by Ben Edwards, the costumes were designed by Jane Greenwood, and the production stage manager was Peter Lawrence. The cast, in order of appearance, was as follows:

IRENE PORTER .... *Colleen Dewhurst*

DAN CONNALLY .... *George Hearn*

JERRY LEEDS .... *Rex Robbins*

PLACE: Irene Porter's apartment on New York City's Upper West Side.

TIME: The present.

ACT ONE

PROLOGUE: The night before the Congressional Election.

SCENE 1: The night of the Congressional Election—3 A.M.

SCENE 2: The following morning.

ACT TWO

Later that evening.

3

An Almost Perfect Person

PROLOGUE

The curtain rises to discover IRENE PORTER *standing at a podium. She is a vital, vibrant woman who possesses enormous reserves of warmth, wit and intelligence.*

The podium is covered with red, white and blue bunting, American flags, and posters advertising her candidacy for the 41st Congressional District, the Upper West Side of New York City. Behind her are a huge, blown-up photograph of IRENE PORTER, *more bunting and flags, and a large sign reading "IRENE PORTER." She is flooded with hot, white television lights, and her podium is covered with microphones.*

IRENE PORTER *is making her final speech of this Congressional campaign. It is the night before the election and she is at campaign headquarters. She speaks directly to the audience, using them as her supporters.*

IRENE. My friends, three months ago, I ran against Morton Davis in the Democratic Primary, and I won. Tomorrow, in the General Election, I run against Morton Davis again, and we are going to win again!

When I first ran against Morton Davis, a thousand speeches ago—"they" said—the nay-sayers said—"It's a lost cause, lady, forget it." When I won the Democratic Primary, they said, "That's what makes Democ-

5

racy work." They also said that Morton would come home and retire. Morton came home. Mad. By the time he reached the Lincoln Tunnel—Morton Davis drove into that tunnel a defeated Democrat, and he drove out a fighting Republican. We turned a seventy-one year old Democrat into a seventy-two year old Republican. And, my friends, I say *that's* Democracy at work!

We're going to win again tomorrow because after twenty-six years in Washington, Morton Davis has developed a bad habit. He has a terrible absentee record. Not from Congress, but from us. We're a nice place to visit, but he doesn't really live here anymore. Morton sees our skyline and he says, "That's our city." We ride our subways and I say, *"That's* our city, and I don't like it." We need a Federal program for Mass Transit, and we need it now! We spend three times more money on welfare payments than we do to teach our children to read. We need Federal Welfare Reform, and we need it now! The Congress of the United States has a committee for everything *except* the needs of the cities. We need that committee, and we need it now!

I am not going to promise you that the day after I am elected we shall have safe streets and unpolluted skies. I'm not even going to promise you that someday we may finish the West Side Highway. But I am going to promise you one thing. When I'm in Washington, I won't forget you. I live here. I'm with you.

I thank you. I love you. Now get out and vote!

(*The lights blackout as the curtain falls.*)

ACT ONE

SCENE 1

The curtain rises on the living room of IRENE PORTER'S *apartment on the Upper West Side of New York City. It is a duplex apartment on the first and second floors of a turn-of-the-century brownstone. The living room is dominated by a staircase connecting the two floors. The furniture is comfortable and eclectic.*

On the Stage Right wall is a large window which overlooks a small courtyard and a thin, but determined tree. A buffet table stands just Onstage of the window, and further Onstage is a dining table with four chairs. Above the table hangs a rather plain chandelier. Just Upstage of the window is a counter unit, which also serves as a bar. It is filled with dishes and glasses below, and liquor bottles and more glasses above. On it is a small lamp. Upstage Right is a door leading to the kitchen. A "Mom-Cat" poster hangs on the door.

The Upstage wall is exposed brick and is divided by the staircase. To the Right of the staircase is a floor-to-ceiling bookcase, filled to over-flowing with books—law books, novels, children's books, stacks of periodicals, encyclopedias, dictionaries, and political biographies. All the books have been read; none are for decoration. On the bookcase hangs a sign, made from a bedsheet and obviously painted by children, reading, "OUR MOM THE WINNER!"

Below the staircase is a huge desk, covered with files, bills, campaign literature, telephone books, a telephone and a reading lamp. Behind the desk, the brick wall is hung with pictures—family photos, political heroes and blow-ups of IRENE *with various political figures.*

The staircase ends on a low landing, which connects with the front door, forming a foyer area. On the Upstage wall, to the Left of the staircase, are coat-hooks bolted into the brick on which hang the winter coats, scarves and toys of IRENE'S *two children, Jenny and Paul. The area below the hooks is filled with ice skates, roller skates, skate boards, hockey sticks, football and baseball equipment, and various games.*

The front door, Upstage Left, opens onto the landing. Beyond the door is an iron gate, open, leading to steps, which in turn, lead up to the sidewalk. IRENE'S *first floor is slightly below street level, and the entrance to her front door is under the stoop of the brownstone. Her apartment is very much in contact with the street life of the Upper West Side.*

In the middle of the Stage Left wall are two windows filled with plants and forming a sort of bay. These windows are shuttered, even though the shutters are open, and the windows have bars on them. Below the windows are radiators covered with decorative grillwork.

Center Stage is an over-stuffed armchair. To its Left is a print sofa with lots of comfortable-looking cushions. The sofa is flanked by a ceramic ele-

phant and a low, antique chest both of which serve as end tables. Behind the sofa is a table with a lamp and a picture of "Joe," IRENE's deceased husband. Stage Left is another armchair; beside it is a small table on which is a telephone.

The apartment is fully carpeted. An oriental rug sits under the sofa and armchairs to form a grouping.

It is 3 A.M. on the night after the election.

When the curtain rises on this room, it is the scene of a party that has just ended. Dirty glasses, filled ashtrays, empty bottles, ravaged food platters, dirty plates, political posters, red, white and blue streamers, and balloons are everywhere. Extra chairs have been set up facing the Television. This was to have been a victory party.

The lights are off, but the Television is on, casting an eerie blue light over the room.

As the curtain rises, over the Television, we hear . . .

IRENE. (*Recorded, coming over the Television.*) My friends, we've run out of beer, we've run out of sandwiches, and we've run out of time. I have just called Morton Davis and congratulated him on his victory tonight. It was a good fight and a close one and we lost—I lost—an election. But we didn't lose. We made a good man angry enough to come home again, to listen to us again, to care again. That's what my politics, people's politics, are all about.

(*The door buzzer rings, impatiently, several times. Then the front door opens admitting* DAN

CONNALLY. *He is* IRENE'S *campaign manager—a tough political professional with an easy Irish charm.*)

DAN. (*Seeing no one in the living room, he calls up the stairs.*) Irene? Reeny?

IRENE. (*Recorded, coming over the Television.*) There are gains for all our losses.

IRENE. (*From upstairs.*) Dan?

IRENE. (*Recorded, coming over the Television.*) There are balms for all our pains. Thank you . . . Thank you . . . Thank you . . . (DAN *crosses to the Television, turning on the living room lights en route.*)

STUDIO ANNOUNCER. (*Recorded, coming over the Television.*) Back to our final returns on the big board, in Nassau County, Norman Lent, Republican is the winner . . . (DAN *changes channels angrily.*)

IRENE. (*Recorded, coming over the Television.*) There are gains for all our losses. There are balms for all our pains. Thank you . . .

(IRENE *appears at the top of the stairs. Unlike the coifed and suited candidate we saw at the pre-election rally, she is now in disarray. Her blouse is out, shoes are off, hair is coming down. She will not show how much this loss has hurt her.*)

IRENE. Thank you . . .

IRENE. (*Recorded, coming over the Television.*) Thank you . . .

IRENE. (*Coming down the stairs.*) Thank you . . .

IRENE. (*Recorded, coming over the Television.*) Thank you. (DAN *turns off the sound, but not the picture on the Television.*)

IRENE. Thank you.

DAN. Three in the morning and they're still running your concession speech. Does that tell you anything?

IRENE. I'm unique. In the year of the woman, in a Democratic sweep, I am the only woman and the only Democrat in the entire five boroughs of New York who lost.

DAN. You had to lose to be on every channel.

IRENE. (*Looking on top of desk for her First Aid Kit.*) The party's over, Dan. Why did you come back?

DAN. You bounce off that screen, you could sell anything. The perfect candidate. (*Turning to her.*) I came back to tell you . . .

IRENE. Better luck next time?

DAN. (*She has been wounded enough today. This is not the time to tell her.*) You forgot to lock the door. You realize anyone could have walked in here?

IRENE. (*Crossing to the bureau, looking for the Kit.*) Except someone with good news. Go home, Dan. There's no campaign to manage anymore. So, please, no instructions. I have done everything I was supposed to do.

DAN. Except win.

IRENE. (*Staring out the window.*) It rained. It rained all day. And when the polls closed, it stopped raining.

DAN. I don't like the way you're taking this.

IRENE. I'm taking this very well. All night people patted me. They patted me like I'd shrunk, and they said, "Irene, you are taking this very well."

DAN. (*Turning off the Television.*) The election is over, Reeny.

IRENE. (*Crossing to the desk.*) This was my winning suit. I wore it when I won the Primary. I wore it when I voted today. I can't even give it to Goodwill. It's bad luck.

DAN. Losing hurts. Yell, Reeny, why don't you yell?

IRENE. (*Finding the Kit in a desk drawer and removing a flannel cloth.*) I can't yell. I wanted to give the people a voice, and I lost mine. For your throat, is it cold compresses or hot? I can't remember what my mother said.

DAN. (*Crossing to bar for a drink.*) My mother said, "Jack Daniels. On the rocks."

IRENE. (*Crossing to table and plunging the cloth into the ice bucket, which now contains mostly water.*) That's cold.

DAN. You still don't understand, do you?

IRENE. Understand what?

DAN. There was no way I could lose this election.

IRENE. You didn't.

DAN. I never lost an election before!

IRENE. You weren't running. I was running! (*She tries to wring out the cloth, but her hand is too sore.*)

DAN. In the last six years, I have managed five campaigns—two Senators, one Governor, one black Mayor, and an honest District Attorney in Baltimore. I won all of them. (*He takes cloth from her, wrings it out with a vengeance and drops it in her hand.*)

IRENE. (*Sitting at dining table and trying to tie cloth around her neck.*) You have nothing to be ashamed of. Everyone outside this room thinks *I* lost.

DAN. (*Tying cloth for her.*) Well, it doesn't matter whether you win or lose. So long as you get elected.

IRENE. (*Defensively.*) I won the Primary my way.

DAN. (*Crossing to sofa with drink.*) You won the Primary because Morton Davis was off trout fishing in Jackson Hole. You lost the election your way.

IRENE. It was close.

DAN. They don't pay off on "close." You still think they walk into that booth, close the curtain, and care. They don't. They buy. You want grass roots? (*He points to the Television set.*) That's where you find them. You want mass votes, you use mass media.

IRENE. Mass media costs mass money.

DAN. Money is the name of the game. You and your damn coffee klatches. You waste two hours on twenty women to raise twenty bucks. A thousand bucks is all anyone is allowed to give. At least get that! And if you can't get it, borrow it!

IRENE. (*Getting an elastic bandage from First Aid Kit.*) I told you in the beginning, I was not going to wake up when this was over, over my head in debt.

DAN. (*He begins to read the newspaper, very much at home.*) If you're in up to your ankles, you may as well go in over your head.

IRENE. Over your head, you drown.

DAN. You swim— And you win!

IRENE. (*Wrapping bandage on her leg.*) I wanted to prove it was possible in this country to win an election without being sold on sixty-second commercials.

DAN. Thirty seconds. I couldn't afford sixty seconds.

IRENE. I wanted to prove it was possible in this country to win on the issues—not the image.

DAN. Well, you learned something.

IRENE. What?

DAN. You were wrong.

IRENE. To lose is wrong. Right? Wrong. To lose is un-American. No citizen shall be deprived of life, liberty, or the right to be a winner. It's the Eleventh Commandment—Thou Shalt Not Fail! There are worse things in this world, Mister, than losing. (*Pause.*) I can't think of one of them right now. Damn it, I hate losing, but I will cry on my own time, and I WASN'T WRONG! (*She slams her hand down on the table in frustration.*) Oh, my God . . .

DAN. Watch the hand. Are you all right? Is it all right?

IRENE. It gave up a week ago. I think it's atrophied. It won't bend.

DAN. I told you you were crazy. I told you you can't shake a hundred thousand hands.

IRENE. What have I got for bringing my message to the streets? A left hand size seven and a right hand size nine.

DAN. The hell with politics. For every winner tonight, there's a loser with a sore throat and a swollen hand.

IRENE. (*She looks at* DAN, *who has been a fact in her life for months, but is now here for no apparent reason.*) What are you doing here? You left. Why didn't you leave?

DAN. (*Putting down the newspaper and rising.*) I came back to tell you . . .

IRENE. What?

DAN. (*He still can't tell her.*) Jerry Leeds will be here at eleven to go over the campaign finances. I forgot to tell you.

IRENE. You told me.

DAN. (*Snapping at her.*) All right. I forgot I told you.

IRENE. Oh, Dan. I worked so hard.

DAN. (*Softening, he crosses to* IRENE *and kisses her on the cheek.*) I'm sorry. That's what I came back to tell you. (*He starts toward the front door.*)

IRENE. Don't go.

DAN. It's late.

IRENE. Talk to me. Not politics. Is there life after an election?

DAN. (*Taking off his coat and hanging it up.*) Normal life for normal people.

IRENE. What do "normal" people talk about?

DAN. The weather. God, it rained all day!

IRENE. That's politics.

DAN. (*Crossing to sofa and sitting.*) Who's sleeping with whom.

IRENE. That's sex.

DAN. That's what normal people talk about.

IRENE. Sex and politics?

DAN. Who's in and who's out.

IRENE. (*Needling, but gently.*) Where's Joanna?

DAN. Joanna?

IRENE. You left here with Joanna Paley, dedicated volunteer and speed typist.

DAN. She worked her heart out over our position papers.

IRENE. She was wearing a bare midriff. In November.

DAN. I took her home.

IRENE. Why?

DAN. I didn't want to win while you were losing.

IRENE. (*Matter-of-fact. Not provocatively.*) Dan, let's go to bed.

DAN. If I could sleep, do you think I'd be here?

IRENE. (*Clarifying as best she can.*) To bed . . . Tonight . . . Together.

DAN. This election really meant a lot to you, didn't it?

IRENE. Dan, look at me! Read Masters and Johnson. I'm at my sexual peak!

DAN. (*Completely off-balance, he automatically relies on the clichéd excuses used on him over the years.*) We're friends. We're good friends.

IRENE. (*Her answers are direct. She doesn't know how to play sexual games.*) I would not ask a stranger.

DAN. What would you say to me tomorrow?

IRENE. Thank you.

DAN. The children. What about the children?

IRENE. Children?

DAN. Your children. Jenny . . . (*He points to the banner.*) "Our Mom The Winner!" Do you know how long she spent making that? Hours. And Paul stuffed literature under five hundred apartment doors today.

IRENE. I love my children.

DAN. Asleep . . . In their beds . . . Upstairs.

IRENE. At my mother's where you dropped them after we left headquarters.

DAN. (*Having found a "safe" subject, pursues it. He also needs a drink and crosses to the bar for it.*) They'll be all right. Don't worry about them. Jenny was crying, but Paul was taking it like a man.

IRENE. What does that mean?

DAN. It means he wasn't crying.

IRENE. Men cry. My husband, Paul's father, he cried and he was a man. He cried at weddings and old movies and when he died I couldn't stop crying. Oh, Joe, why did you have to go and die on me? (DAN *reaches out to her. She wants no sympathy and crosses away from him.*) I'm sorry. I should have known better. All the time I've known you, I've never seen you in public with anyone over twenty-five.

DAN. (*Sitting at the table.*) Joanna's thirty-two.

IRENE. You'd never know it. With that bare midriff. In November.

DAN. Knock it off, Reeny. You're a damned attractive woman.

IRENE. Widow. (*She looks out the windows.*)

DAN. I just . . . It's late and I admit, I never thought of you . . . Of course, I've thought of you, but not that way . . . that is, not recently . . .

IRENE. (*Turning to* DAN.) When?

DAN. Look, when you work closely with someone you respect, you don't mix business with pleasure.

IRENE. (*Crossing down to the sofa.*) Why not?

DAN. Because the pleasure screws up the business.

IRENE. Our business is screwed up, and we haven't had any pleasure.

DAN. (*Defensively.*) I can't perform on demand.

IRENE. Demand? I made a suggestion. You made suggestions—"Mass Media" and I said, "No." Now, I made a suggestion, and you said, "No." We're even. No hard feelings. (*She crosses to him and shakes his hand, forgetting her own injured hand.*) Oh, my God, no . . . (*She crosses away from him in pain. He comes to her and begins to massage her wounded hand.*) I did it all wrong, didn't I? I don't know how to do it. I mean . . . across a crowded room, smiles and small talk. There are women, I know them, I watch them. She looks and he looks and she knows and he knows and she *knows* that he knows and . . . I CAN'T DANCE!

DAN. I know.

IRENE. I didn't take dancing lessons. I took flute lessons. If I could dance, my whole life would be different. How do you know?

DAN. Where did we meet?

IRENE. It was a lifetime ago.

DAN. (*Crossing to the table for his drink.*) Six months ago. An N.D.C. fund raiser at the Biltmore Hotel. I asked you to dance.

IRENE. And I made one of my usual excuses . . .

DAN. You said, "I don't dance." Porelli introduced us.

IRENE. I asked him to. I said, "Tony, who's the best?" He said, "Sweetheart, best wins. See that guy sitting over there? He's got himself a hotshot P.R. business in Washington, but, if you can get him, he knows how to run a campaign."

DAN. We sat at the bar and you laid this campaign on me chapter and verse. They closed up around us. Put the chairs up on the tables.

IRENE. You were a hard sell.

DAN. I said yes.

IRENE. You thought about it for three days. Then you said yes.

DAN. It's not like a marriage. You don't just plunge in.

IRENE. When I asked Joe to marry me, he said yes, just like . . .

DAN. (*Snapping his fingers.*) Like that?

IRENE. If I were Catholic, I wouldn't confess that.

DAN. (*Sitting at the table.*) It's not a mortal sin.

IRENE. We lived together for two years before we were married.

DAN. That's five Hail Mary's.

IRENE. (*Crossing away from* DAN, *remembering.*) In those days, you didn't just come right out and live together. He was getting his Ph.D. and I was at N.Y.U. Law, and he had three roommates and I lived at home. On a big Saturday night, he'd borrow a car and we'd stop by a deli and pick up roast beef sandwiches and pickles and beer and a box of chocolate doughnuts and we'd drive over the George Washington Bridge. We'd check into one of those motels—right across the bridge. And then we'd go in and have our sandwiches and pickles and beer . . . And we'd save our chocolate doughnuts . . . (*To* DAN *and back to the present.*) It was very nice. Jerry introduced us.

DAN. Jerry Leeds?

IRENE. Jerry Leeds is my oldest friend. We grew up together. We lived in the same apartment building.

DAN. The boy next door.

IRENE. Upstairs. He was the best man at my wedding. The day I graduated from law school, I proposed to Joe. (DAN *snaps his fingers.*) It was a good marriage. We had fourteen years and two children and I like my in-laws and I never cheated and he died. October. October 10th. It was two years. (*She sits on the sofa.*)

DAN. Two years . . . Two years and you haven't . . . (*He makes a subtly suggestive gesture.*)

IRENE. Of course, I have. (*Pause.*) No, I haven't.

DAN. Reeny, it's not healthy.

IRENE. Celibacy is not a disease.

DAN. (*Rising.*) You're a Reform Democrat!

IRENE. I've been busy. I cried for one year and I ran for Congress the next.

DAN. What about that doctor who kept hanging around headquarters?

IRENE. Marvin Stern? Periodontist.

DAN. Perio . . . ?

IRENE. Gums. Great Neck.

DAN. I always thought . . .

IRENE. I never asked him.

DAN. (*Sitting in the armchair.*) One day, Reeny, do yourself a favor. Let someone ask you.

IRENE. I can't. It's the way I was brought up. As long as I can remember, my father told me, "In this world, Reeny, if you want something, ask for it. What's the worst thing that can happen? They say, 'No.' "

DAN. And when they say no?

IRENE. He was a judge. He said, "Re-phrase the question." (*Both laugh.*) The children brought me a bottle of champagne. Will you have a drink with me?

DAN. Reeny . . .

IRENE. (*Rising.*) Nolo contendere. Case dismissed. Well?

DAN. (*Rising.*) My father owned a bar in Queens. He said, "Never turn down a free drink." (*She crosses to kitchen door.*) Reeny, when I dance, I lead. It's the way I was brought up.

IRENE. (*Looking at the banner.*) I have to take *that* down. (*She exits into kitchen.*)

DAN. If there were any justice in this world, which

there isn't, you should have won big! (*He crosses to Television set and snaps it on.*)

ED RIOS. (*Recorded, coming over the Television.*) In Queens, Benjamin Rosenthal returns to Congress for his eighth term. In the ninth Congressional District, it is James Delaney, the winner, his sixteenth term. In the Bronx, an easy victory for Mario Biaggi on the Democratic and Republican lines. (TELEVISION ANNOUNCER *continues throughout as needed. See APPENDIX.*)

ED RIOS. (*Continued.*) And in Brooklyn, Shirley Chisholm has no trouble retaining her seat. Charles Rangle has a clean sweep in the nineteenth, and in Manhattan, in the forty-first, it is now, Irene Porter the winner over incumbent Morton Davis.

IRENE. (*Enters with champagne and glasses.*) Do we have to listen to the last rites?

DAN. It's Ed Rios.

IRENE. What did he say?

DAN. (*Simultaneously.*) Did you hear what he said?

IRENE. I see it!

DAN. (*Running to Television set.*) Look!

IRENE. (*Stunned.*) I won ... I won, I won, I won ...

DAN. I won it! I did it!

IRENE. (*Crossing to table.*) Winner. I am a winner, winner, winner!

DAN. I was right! Oh, was I right! I knew it was there. I knew I could take it and I took it. I won it!

IRENE. (*To* DAN.) *I* won it!

DAN. I did it!

IRENE. Over here! Winner!

DAN. Follow the instincts! Go with the gut!

IRENE. (*Running to sofa and standing on it.*) Look at a winner!

DAN. Not 'til the last vote's counted. I knew I could do it. And I went right out and I did it and, by God, I won it!

IRENE. *I* won . . . *I* won, *I* won, *I* won, *I,I,I,I,I* . . . *I WON!* (*She throws a glass in anger. It breaks on the stairs.*)

DAN. *YOU WON!*

IRENE. We won . . . WE WON! (*They embrace.*) Where's the board?

DAN. They've gone past.

IRENE. Roll it back! (DAN *crosses to Television. She orates.*) Victory has a hundred fathers! Defeat is an orphan!

DAN. What?

IRENE. My acceptance speech. I go the House of Representatives at your will. It is from your streets that I come. It is at your side that I stand. My friends . . . (DAN *switches channels, and from the Television the sign-off music of "The Star-Spangled Banner" fills the air.* IRENE *sings fervently . . .*) "Oh, say can you see, by the dawn's early light . . ."

DAN. (*Switching channels once more.*) He's back! (*Goes to the telephone to dial, check it out.*)

ED RIOS. (*Recorded, coming over the Television.*) . . . numbers were right but the slot was wrong. In the 41st C.D., the correct return—a final. Morton Davis, the winner, over Irene Porter. Davis, in the Republican and Liberal columns, 41,133 votes. (DAN *hangs up the phone.*) Mrs. Porter, 39,274 . . . (IRENE *crumbles down onto the sofa.*)

DAN. (*Switching off the Television and crossing away from her to table.*) I should have known. When do I learn?

IRENE. By accident, Paul broke his arm and by accident, I was in politics. I'm a damned good attorney.

That's what I do. But Paul fell off a swing when he was three and broke his arm—here and here—because under the swing the surface was cement. I organized the mothers and we petitioned City Hall. We rallied and pressured and when we were through, we had a whole new playground. We feel helpless in this city. There's a welfare hotel two blocks down, across the street. Don't look at it. Walk this side of the street. I make Paul carry a dollar in his pocket—just in case. It's "give up and don't get hurt" money. I'm right. I don't want him hurt. But it's wrong. I was born here and brought up here and I'm going to stay here and raise my children here because I love this dirty, disgusting, humiliating, *beautiful* city. It didn't matter, did it? Paul broke his arm in two places and I tried very hard and it didn't matter. It didn't mean shit. (*She rises and crosses to the stairs.*)

DAN. Don't step on the . . . (*She steps on a shard of glass.*)

IRENE. Shit, shit, shit, shit, shit, SHIT!

DAN. (*Crossing to help her.*) . . . glass.

IRENE. I am bleeding. I am bleeding. I am dying, Egypt!

DAN. (*Helping her to sofa.*) Calm down. Let me look . . .

IRENE. I can't look. It's an open wound.

DAN. (*Examining her foot.*) It's a splinter.

IRENE. Call an ambulance.

DAN. What do I tell them?

IRENE. Tell them I'm hysterical! Tell them I'm having a breakdown. Tell them I have just lost an election, twice! And I am entitled to one decent everyday nervous breakdown!

DAN. (*Pulling out the piece of glass.*) Hold still. I've . . . got it. (*Looking in First Aid Kit.*) Iodine?

IRENE. Bactine.

DAN. (*He takes out the can and shakes it.*) Empty. (*Throwing the can back into the Kit.*)

IRENE. Of course, it's empty. How could you think it would be anything *but* empty?

DAN. (*Reaching for the champagne bottle.*) Will you relax a minute?

IRENE. I need a tetanus shot! My voice is gone. My hand won't move. My leg is stiff. Now gangrene is going to set in and I'm going to lose my foot.

DAN. (*Opening the champagne.*) Anything else?

IRENE. What's worse than losing your foot?

DAN. (*Pouring champagne on a napkin and putting the napkin on her cut.*) You could lose the election three times tonight.

IRENE. What are you doing?

DAN. Antiseptic.

IRENE. That's my champagne!

DAN. "There are gains for all our losses. There are balms for all our pains."

IRENE. Who said that?

DAN. You did.

IRENE. I didn't.

DAN. Your concession speech.

IRENE. Oh, my God . . . (*Taking champagne bottle and raising it in a toast.*) To Adlai Stevenson. May he forgive me. (*She drinks from the bottle.*)

DAN. Better? (*She drinks again.*) To hell with it, Reeny. It's not a good time to be alone. Let's go upstairs.

IRENE. Upstairs?

DAN. Up the stairs . . .

IRENE. You and me?

DAN. To bed . . . Tonight . . . Together . . .

IRENE. Oh, Dan, that's . . . kind.

DAN. We shall comfort each other.

IRENE. I can't.

DAN. What do you mean, you can't?

IRENE. I can't.

DAN. Why not?

IRENE. Because you haven't asked me. You said it. You told me, "Someday, Reeny, let somebody ask you!"

DAN. I'm asking!

IRENE. You're not!

DAN. Reeny, will you go to bed with me?!

IRENE. I don't think I remember how any more . . .

DAN. It's like riding a bicycle. Once you learn, you never forget.

IRENE. I can't ride a bicycle! (*They both laugh.*)

DAN. Irene, will you please go to bed with me?

IRENE. You're feeling sorry for me.

DAN. (*Rising. Enough of this new game-playing.*) You may be an expert on the problems of New York City, but when it comes to men, you don't know shit from apple butter. And when it comes to Irishmen . . .

IRENE. Here comes the brogue . . .

DAN. No, no! Listen, my father was no judge. He poured an honest drink, cracked heads when he had to and Sunday lunch, he did not say Grace. He read us a selection from the collected works of Mister Dooley. He named his pub after him because Mr. Dooley knew his politics, and he knew his people. "We're a simple people," the good man said, "Simple like th' air or the deep green sea. Not complicated like a watch that stops when the suit iv clothes ye got it with wears out." But stubborn as cart mules! Now stand up. And move!

IRENE. (*She stands and limps a few steps.*) I can't move. I can't walk! (*He crosses to her and begins to pick her up.*) Dan, you can't carry me upstairs!

DAN. If I like it, I'll carry you downstairs!

IRENE. If *I* like it, you won't have the strength! (*She crosses to the stairs.* DAN *follows.*) Dan, are you sure?

DAN. I think . . . that's why I came back.

IRENE. I think . . . that's why I didn't lock the door. (*They both climb several steps.* DAN *turns.*)

DAN. Reeny, look down there.

IRENE. (*Looking at the mess from the party.*) I can't clean it up now.

DAN. If Davis had done the decent thing and retired after the Primary, if you'd won, where would we be?

IRENE. Down there.

DAN. (*His tone says, "And politics as usual."*) With the phones going and the hangers-on . . .

IRENE. (*Her commitment rising to the surface.*) And a purpose. I'd be out of politics and into government.

DAN. (*Almost to himself.*) "Tread softly, because you tread on my dreams . . ."

IRENE. What's that?

DAN. That's Yeats. It's over, Reeny.

IRENE. I know it's over. I'm better. I'm going to be just fine. (*He starts upstairs. She stops him.*) Dan, I wear bras and Ace bandages. I have two Caesarian scars. And the only thing I can do with my right hand is salute. (*He takes her hand lovingly and leads her up the stairs as . . .*)

THE CURTAIN FALLS

ACT ONE

SCENE 2

Over the loudspeakers in the house, the following recorded telephone conversation is heard. CHUCK'S *voice is filtered, as if his voice were coming through the telephone, while* JERRY'S *voice is present, as if he were in the room.*

A telephone rings three times. Sound of telephone receiver being picked up.

CHUCK. Irene Porter For Congress Headquarters.

JERRY. Chuck, that was yesterday.

CHUCK. It's a habit. Jerry?

JERRY. Yeah. Have you got a pencil and paper? Here's the schedule for closing up headquarters. Number one, the phone company. They say they'll be there to take the phones out between twelve and five. That means wait until six and expect them tomorrow. Two. I found a "Save The Environment" group to take all the campaign literature and the posters. They're happy to have something to recycle. Three. Harry, the used furniture man. He's sending a truck, and he takes everything. Empty the filing cabinets, but make sure you save the contributor cards. Put 'em all in those shoe boxes I brought in.

CHUCK. She's not thinking about running again?

JERRY. Running again? I'm thinking about paying off the deficit. We'll send out a mailing. Who knows? Maybe someone will send in a condolence check. (*The curtain rises to find* JERRY LEEDS *sitting on the edge of the desk involved in a telephone conversation with* CHUCK; *his briefcase is open and in front of him.* JERRY LEEDS *is* IRENE'S *oldest and dearest friend. He is an organized and efficient C.P.A. with a loving sense of humor, but he is a bit at sea in the modern world. A miraculous transformation has taken place in the living room. Gone is all the debris from last night's party. The furniture has been re-arranged, the extra chairs have been folded and neatly stacked against the wall, and sunlight floods the apartment. The only remnant* of the "victory" party is the "OUR MOM THE WINNER!" banner, which still hangs on the bookcase. JERRY, *speaking into the telephone.*) Don't be depressed. What have you got to be depressed about? All you have to do is close up headquarters. I have to tell her she owes seventy-five thousand dollars in campaign debt . . . You're right. Life is hell. Accept that, and you're never disappointed. I'll see you later. (*He hangs up the phone. He checks his watch, crosses to the stairs and looks up. Seeing no signs of activity, he crosses toward the kitchen and sees the "OUR MOM THE WINNER!" banner still hanging on the bookcase.*) Our Mom. The Winner. (*He pulls down the banner and folds it as one would fold an American flag taken from a hero's coffin. Putting the folded banner on the bookcase, he exits into the kitchen.*)

IRENE. (*From upstairs, singing the Star-Spangled Banner, slowly, sensually.*) "Oh, say can you see, by the dawn's early light, what so proudly we hailed . . ." (*She comes slowly down the stairs, dressed in a slightly outrageous blue peignoir, and sees the immaculate living room.*) Thank you . . . Thank you . . . Thank you.

JERRY. (*Entering from the kitchen.*) You're welcome.

IRENE. Jerry? (*Then she remembers.*) Jerry. Campaign finances. 11 o'clock. What time is it?

JERRY. 12:06.

IRENE. (*She comes down off the stairs.*) I'm sorry . . .

JERRY. You needed the sleep. Watch out. There was glass all over the place. Some nut went crazy last night. If I told you once, in politics, use plastic.

IRENE. (*Going into kitchen.*) Where's Dan?

JERRY. Dan's in Washington.

IRENE. (*Coming out of kitchen.*) Washington?

JERRY. Irene, what did he say last night?

IRENE. He said a lot of things last night. I don't remember Washington.

JERRY. He had to be in Washington this morning on business.

IRENE. (*Crossing to bay windows to check plants.*) Washington . . . ?

JERRY. (*Concerned.*) Irene, how do you feel?

IRENE. (*Expansively.*) Oh, Jerry, I feel . . .

JERRY. I know. Angry, miserable and rejected.

IRENE. (*Amused; coming to* JERRY.) Jerry, think of it. I was not shaking hands at a subway station at 7 o'clock this morning. I don't have to stand in the garment district this afternoon and eat a cold potato knish, and above all, I do not have to end up at midnight being re-scheduled for tomorrow. What am I going to do all day?

JERRY. First, you're going to sit down and have a cup of coffee.

IRENE. (*She starts toward kitchen.*) I'll make it.

JERRY. (*Stopping her and taking her to sofa.*) No. I made it. It's made. I made the arrangements to close up headquarters. I cleaned up the house, I made the coffee, and I stopped by Zabar's and picked up some Russian cake.

IRENE. Ten minutes more and you would have washed the windows.

JERRY. They can use it. (*He exits into kitchen.*)

IRENE. Jerry . . .

JERRY. What?

IRENE. Who let you in?

JERRY. I let me in. When Joe died, you gave me a key for emergencies.

IRENE. That was two years ago.

JERRY. (*Entering from kitchen carrying a tray with coffee, cups and coffee cake.*) It still fits. I rang. You didn't answer. It could have been an emergency.

IRENE. Jerry, all I lost was an election.

JERRY. (*Setting the tray on the coffee table.*) That's not quite accurate. (*The telephone rings.* IRENE *answers it.*)

IRENE. Hello? . . . Yes, this is she. (JERRY *brings her coffee; to* JERRY:) It's Ed Rios. To apologize. (*The desk telephone rings.* JERRY *crosses to answer it.*) That's my mother. It's the private line.

JERRY. (*On phone.*) Hello, Irma?

IRENE. (*To* JERRY.) Tell her I'll call her back.

JERRY. (*On phone.*) It's Jerry, how are you?

IRENE. (*On phone.*) Hello, Ed?

JERRY. Irene slept. Until noon.

IRENE. How could I sleep? I was listening to you all night. Win. Lose. Win. Lose.

JERRY. She's talking to Ed Rios.

IRENE. Don't apologize. To err is human.

JERRY. They're fine and you'll pick them up after school . . . I'll tell her . . . No, I promise . . . You take care now. (*He hangs up.*)

IRENE. (*To* JERRY.) He wants to do a special. The aftermath. What it costs to lose. Emotionally. Financially. (*On the phone.*) Edward, under the Corrupt Practices Act, I am a model of fiscal decorum. (*To* JERRY.) The bottom line?

JERRY. (*Gathering his ledger and papers from his briefcase.*) That's what we're meeting about.

IRENE. Give me a rough figure.

JERRY. (*Crossing to* IRENE *with papers.*) You're on the phone.

IRENE. Jerry, we have to file it anyway.

JERRY. (*Reluctantly.*) In the neighborhood of seventy-five thousand dollars.

IRENE. It could be worse. (*On the phone.*) Ed, seventy thousand is what we budgeted. We spent seventy-five thousand.

JERRY. We *owe*.

IRENE. (*To* JERRY.) We . . . what?

JERRY. Give or take some advertising rebates.

IRENE. I owe seventy-five thousand dollars!?

JERRY. Would I lie to you? Why do you think I was cleaning? (*Taking her coffee cup to tray.*) Watch out! You'll spill.

IRENE. Why didn't you tell me? Why didn't you say something?

JERRY. Ed Rios!

IRENE. My budget!

JERRY. On the news . . . On the phone . . .

IRENE. (*Into phone.*) Hello, Ed? Are you there? Yes, something is going on. Emotionally and financially. Ed, please . . . let me get back to you . . . (*She hangs up.*) Seventy-five thousand dollars . . .

JERRY. Give or take . . . (*The telephone rings.*)

IRENE. Start. At the beginning.

JERRY. The phone . . .

IRENE. Let it ring.

JERRY. Three weeks ago . . . I can't let it ring.

IRENE. (*Picking up the telephone and immediately hanging it up.*) It is not ringing. Three weeks ago . . . WHAT HAPPENED?

JERRY. (*Sitting on sofa.*) It was your mother before. The kids are fine.

IRENE. Good.

JERRY. They went to school. She's going to pick them up after school.

IRENE. Good.

(*The telephone rings.* IRENE *picks up the telephone—it is a modular push-button unit. She detaches the back cord, thus disconnecting it totally. She then replaces the telephone on the table.*)

JERRY. You don't have to call her back.

IRENE. (*Rising.*) What happened three weeks ago!

JERRY. We made a calculated decision . . .

IRENE. To spend seventy-five thousand dollars without mentioning it!

JERRY. It didn't start that way. It grew. It ended that way.

IRENE. Do you know how much money that is?

JERRY. Irene, be reasonable. It takes a million dollars a week to run for President.

IRENE. I was running for the 41st Congressional District. That's not even a silk stocking district. It's orthopedic shoes!

JERRY. Morton Davis outspent us three to one.

IRENE. (*Crossing to table.*) Where did it go?

JERRY. Television time.

IRENE. (*The worst possible thing.*) Television time!

JERRY. We put everything we could beg, borrow—we didn't steal, Irene—into more television time. You needed the exposure.

IRENE. Where's Dan? Where is Dan?

JERRY. I told you. In Washington.

IRENE. Washington!

JERRY. You don't know what television time costs . . .

IRENE. Why didn't you tell me?

JERRY. I'm telling you. Thirty seconds on the news—three thousand dollars. That's a hundred dollars a second. For one shot. Local.

IRENE. If I couldn't afford it, how could you authorize it?

JERRY. If you want mass votes, you use mass media.

IRENE. That's not you. That's Dan talking.

JERRY. Dan's the expert.

IRENE. Why didn't the expert tell me?

JERRY. When could he tell you?

IRENE. How about three weeks ago? How about last night?

JERRY. You had enough on your hands last night. It was my job to tell you and I am telling you NOW! (*Pause; then calmly.*) Irene, Dan did it for you and he was right.

IRENE. Don't tell me he was right. Dashing Dan Connally, the professional Celt. He leaves you to bring the news. He leaves me to wake up, over my head in debt, drowning, and where is he? (*Holding up her hand to stop him from telling her.*) Washington! (*A dirge.*) Oh, "Romantic Ireland's dead and gone/It's with O'Leary in the grave."

JERRY. What's that?

IRENE. That's Yeats.

JERRY. (*Crossing to her.*) Irene, we got you into this, and we'll get you out of it. Of course you're upset. It's a perfectly normal female reaction.

IRENE. Female?

JERRY. You are a woman.

IRENE. I am a person. (IRENE *crosses to sofa and sits.*)

JERRY. A female person, and you are vulnerable. (JERRY *sits beside* IRENE.) You are alone, and the bubble burst and . . . the hell with it, Reeny, it's not a good time to be alone. Let's . . .

IRENE. (*A reflex reaction.*) NO!

JERRY. (*Nonplussed.*) Let's . . . talk.

IRENE. Yesterday I ran for Congress. Today I file for welfare.

JERRY. You're eligible. It's a fatherless home. (*Recognizing how tactless that was.*) I'm sorry. I was trying to cheer you up. Cry, Reeny, cry your heart out. You'll feel better.

IRENE. I cried my heart out over Joe. I can't cry my heart out over money.

JERRY. Irene, you're taking this very well. Last night, we all said, "It is amazing how well you're taking this." You know what my grandfather used to say about you? "That's some girl." That's what he used to say. "She's got her head screwed on her shoulders, and she's got her bare feet right on the floor."

IRENE. He never approved.

JERRY. How could he approve? He was in the shoe business. (*They both laugh.*)

IRENE. Oh, Jerry. My family always thought . . . one day . . . you and me . . .

JERRY. So did mine. (*A pause.*) So did I.

IRENE. Jerry, you introduced me to Joe.

JERRY. His head was in the clouds. Your feet were on the floor. I didn't think it would take. Your wedding . . .

IRENE. You were best man.

JERRY. When you put that ring on Joe's finger, I had both rings, do you remember? You looked at me, just for a second. That second I thought, "She's going to do it. She's going to reach past him and put that ring on my finger." You didn't.

IRENE. Jerry, I didn't know. I never ever thought . . .

JERRY. Why would you? I never said anything. I never asked you. I almost did . . .

IRENE. When?

JERRY. When we almost went away skiing to Stowe, for the weekend. Lincoln's birthday, 1951. Before Joe. Before Gloria.

IRENE. I don't remember . . .

JERRY. How can you remember? We never went skiing. I had it all planned. You thought we were going to stay in the dormitories, but I reserved a room. I was going to tell you it was the last room, the only room. The day before we were going to leave . . .

IRENE. (*She remembers.*) You broke your ankle!

JERRY. You remember. I walked into a pothole. My grandfather said it was fate. He said, "Moses walked

down the mountain. He didn't ski down the mountain."
I couldn't tell him that I wanted to stay at the bottom
of the mountain. With you.

IRENE. You really reserved a room?

JERRY. Paid in advance. I lost . . . twenty-two
dollars.

IRENE. (*Sitting forward.*) I lost . . .

JERRY. (*Sitting forward.*) Seventy-five thousand.
That's inflation.

IRENE. You should have asked me, Jerry. I think I
would have said yes.

JERRY. No.

IRENE. Before Joe. Before Gloria. Before . . . the
national debt.

JERRY. We won't think about that. There's time to
think about that. Close your eyes and relax, Reeny. We
won't talk about it, and we won't think about it. (*She
settles back against* JERRY's *shoulder; his arm is
around her. He begins to pat her rhythmically.*)

IRENE. Jerry . . . Hold me, but don't pat me. (*He
stops patting. She closes her eyes. They are still and
relaxed. Then he puts his hands on her breast. Her
eyes open.*) What are you doing?

JERRY. I'm holding you.

IRENE. Don't hold me. Pat me.

JERRY. (*He begins to pat her breast. She removes his
hand and sits up.*) I'm sorry. I didn't mean to . . .

IRENE. What did you mean to do?

JERRY. Nothing. I don't know. Comfort you . . .

IRENE. Comfort! I don't need any more comfort. I've
had enough comfort!

JERRY. What's so terrible about comfort?

IRENE. (*Rising and crossing to table.*) Comfort is
comfort and sex is sex! When comfort is sex, it is not
comfort!

JERRY. I barely put my hand . . .

IRENE. If Morton Davis had lost this election, would his campaign manager have felt him up?

JERRY. I am your finance chairman!

IRENE. (*Crossing to* JERRY.) You gave the eulogy at my husband's funeral. You are the godfather to my children. You are married. You are a model of upwardly mobile marriage. From West End Avenue to Yonkers to Poundridge. That's the American dream and you have it all. You have an immaculate, remodelled, 18th Century farmhouse . . . with the original beams. You have three shining little girls. Above all, you have Gloria, a beautiful, loving wife.

JERRY. A social worker.

IRENE. (*Sitting in armchair.*) She is not a social worker. She just went back to school a year ago.

JERRY. (*Rising and crossing away from* IRENE.) My marriage is falling apart.

IRENE. I always think of you together. Cleaning up.

JERRY. She won't let me near her. She won't let me touch her. We sleep in the same room, in the same bed. We say good night, and we roll over, and I face the wall and she faces the window and . . . we sleep. There is always an excuse. Her homework. Her tennis elbow. The ink on my fingers. If I roll over and touch her—by accident, a mistake, a leg in the night—if I touch her, she jumps. Her whole body suffers an involuntary muscular contraction. I touch. She jumps. I touched you. You jumped. Pavlov lives!

IRENE. (*Her anger forgotten; involved in his problem.*) Why didn't you tell me?

JERRY. I can't talk about it.

IRENE. I should have known. I should have sensed something.

JERRY. Who senses the sex life of a C.P.A.?

IRENE. Jerry, have you tried to get some help?

JERRY. (*Crossing back toward* IRENE.) We went to

a marriage counsellor. He said Gloria's universe is expanding. Mine is contracting. That's the conflict. She's changed, Reeny, since she went back to school. I don't know her. She's not the same person.

IRENE. I'll talk to her. We'll have lunch. I have time to have lunch now.

JERRY. Irene, no. Listen, It's not her fault. It's my fault. I did it. When Tracy, the little one, started first grade—you know, full time—I kept telling her, "Gloria, the house is decorated, the children are in school. Do something with your life." And she did. She doesn't take courses. She takes causes . . . Consciousness raising. Affirmative action. Organic food. I *hate* yogurt! I turned a beautiful, loving wife into a liberated woman.

IRENE. Jerry, I am a liberated woman.

JERRY. You always were. Don't you understand? She converted!

IRENE. (*Crossing to* JERRY.) There has to be something you can do. Something we can do. (*Both sit on sofa.*)

JERRY. On my thirteenth birthday, my grandfather said to my father, "Today, you tell the boy what's what about you know what." And he walked out of the room. My father said to me, "Jerry, someday you'll meet a nice girl, and you'll like her, and she'll like you. You'll get married. You'll go on a honeymoon—on a boat. Then you'll come home and, with a little luck, *I'll* be a grandfather." And *he* walked out of the room. I remember sitting there thinking, "That's what's what about you know what?" You know something? It is.

IRENE. (*Remembering.*) Oh, Jerry, you never know. Sometimes when you least expect it, it can be beautiful. (*Back to reality.*) Then you wake up, and it's over and, what the hell. He's gone. But for a while, it was lovely. It was Mozart.

JERRY. Lucky Joe.

IRENE. Joe?

JERRY. Fourteen years of Mozart.

IRENE. (*Getting her coffee cup.*) Fourteen years . . . (*Deciding to tell him what no one knew.*) I left him once.

JERRY. Who? Joe?

IRENE. Yes.

JERRY. No. When?

IRENE. (*Pouring herself more coffee.*) There was a graduate student. A very young, very attractive graduate student.

JERRY. That was your imagination. Joe wouldn't . . .

IRENE. He wouldn't? He did. What do you call a fight in marriage counsellor language?

JERRY. A confrontation.

IRENE. (*Sitting beside* JERRY *on sofa.*) We had one hell of a confrontation. I wasn't paying attention. The last thing I wanted to believe was that it might, somehow, be my fault, too. So I threw some things in a bag, and stormed out.

JERRY. (*He remembers.*) You flew to Austria. By yourself.

IRENE. I went to Salzburg. The Mozart Festival. Oh, Jerry, it was magical.

JERRY. It "blew your mind" . . . (*She reacts to the phrase. He explains.*) We have a very young marriage counselor.

IRENE. It cleared my mind. I knew we loved each other and that I could come home and say, "Hey, it's not just my life or your life. It's *our* life, too." Sometimes, Jerry, you just have to get away.

JERRY. (*Rising; dealing with this advice.*) Yeah? Yeah! Where'll we go?

IRENE. We?

JERRY. (*Crossing to table.*) The country? The beach?

You just said, "What am I going to do all day?" The mountains! Stowe!

IRENE. No.

JERRY. (*Crossing above sofa.*) Right. That was then. We can go anywhere now. A city! Pick a city. No. Don't pick a city. I've got the city. San Francisco.

IRENE. It's three thousand miles away.

JERRY. We won't see anyone we know. Have you got an extra toothbrush? All I need is a toothbrush. Oh, hell, I'll buy a toothbrush.

IRENE. Jerry, I can't go away with you.

JERRY. Give me one good reason.

IRENE. Gloria.

JERRY. She has midterms.

IRENE. Dan.

JERRY. He's in Washington.

IRENE. The money.

JERRY. Believe me, Irene, debts don't run away.

IRENE. You can't run away with me, Jerry.

JERRY. Yes, I can. It's not tax season!

IRENE. It's responsibility season. It's losers season!

JERRY. (*Nothing can deter him.*) That's right. Today we are both losers! We deserve a vacation!

IRENE. (*Trying to tell him about* DAN.) Last night, Jerry . . . Late last night . . .

JERRY. (*Cutting her off, undeterred.*) Don't tell me about last night, and how many votes, and "they" all love you because "they" don't count. You walked down those stairs today and you were alone. I face that wall every night and so am I. You can't tell me about losing nights, Reeny. I'm the expert.

IRENE. I love you, Jerry, but I can't go away today.

JERRY. (*He pauses, nearly defeated. Then, suddenly.*) We don't have to go away. Who has to go away? We're there.

IRENE. Where?

JERRY. Right here. In San Francisco.

IRENE. It's 84th Street. Between Riverside Drive and West End Avenue . . .

JERRY. (*Sitting beside* IRENE *on sofa.*) No. It's the Fairmont Hotel. You cut off the phone. We're not taking any calls. Room service brought us coffee and a Russian cake. They flew it in . . .

IRENE. All the way from Zabar's?

JERRY. Would I lie to you? Look out the window. Come on, Reeny, just look. What do you see?

IRENE. (*She looks.*) Alcatraz. (*She turns back to* JERRY.)

JERRY. Irene, I made this reservation a long time ago. Now, look out there. A little to the left. (*She turns to window again.*) All my life I've just missed asking you to love me. Irene, what do you see?

IRENE. I see the Bay and the Golden Gate Bridge. Sometimes, Jerry, when you least expect it, it can be . . .

JERRY. Beautiful?

IRENE. Would I lie to you? (*They lean back on the sofa, his arms around her as . . .*)

THE CURTAIN FALLS

ACT TWO

It is later that evening. The living room is dark. As the curtain rises, the loud siren and honking of a fire engine is heard. A key is heard in the front door lock, and the door opens.

JERRY. (*Enters carrying several shoe boxes with contributor cards.*) This key is for emergencies. In two years, I only used it once.

DAN. (*Enters just behind* JERRY *with more boxes of cards; switching on the room lights.*) Well, now you've used it twice. Come on in. (DAN *puts his boxes on desk.*)

JERRY. It's not right to walk into someone's house when she's not here. (JERRY *looks down at his shoe, sees that he has stepped in dog droppings outside, and exits.*)

DAN. (*Not seeing* JERRY *leave.*) She told us to meet her here. How long could we sit in your car with the doors locked guarding the contributors' cards? (*Realizing* JERRY *is outside.*) Jerry? Jerry? (DAN *opens the front door.*)

JERRY. (*Checking his shoe as he enters.*) New York . . .

DAN. (*Hanging up his coat.*) She told me nine o'clock. Did she tell you nine o'clock? (DAN *takes ice bucket and exits into kitchen.*)

JERRY. (*Putting his boxes on desk.*) I told you, she said she had a lot of things to work out today. (*Taking off his coat.*) Then she was having dinner with her mother and the children.

DAN. (*Entering with bucket filled with ice.*) Then she ought to be here any minute. Those kids have got to go to bed.

40

JERRY. (*Hanging up his coat.*) They're staying at her mother's.

DAN. Again?

JERRY. Irene didn't think Irma ought to be alone.

DAN. (*Delighted.*) She's absolutely right. It's not a good time to be alone. (*Fixing himself a drink.*) Do you want a drink?

JERRY. Yes. No. It's cold in here.

DAN. Put your coat on.

JERRY. (*He puts his coat on; he heads for kitchen.*) Oh, yeah. Right. Maybe I'll make some coffee.

DAN. How did she take it?

JERRY. With milk. (*He disappears into kitchen.*)

DAN. The news. The money. The facts of life.

JERRY. (*Re-appears from kitchen.*) The facts of life?

DAN. Are you all right?

JERRY. (*Taking his coat off.*) It's warm in here.

DAN. You explained it all this morning . . . ?

JERRY. This afternoon. I told her everything.

DAN. (*Sitting on sofa.*) How did she take it? And don't tell me with milk.

JERRY. She was . . . perfect.

DAN. She was like a major general on the phone. I told her I was coming back tomorrow but, oh, no, it had to be tonight. I raced for that shuttle and now, where the hell is she?

(JERRY *opens front door, looking for* IRENE. *There is a passing blast of salsa music from a transistor radio. He quickly closes the door.*)

JERRY. This is no place for a woman, alone, to bring up two kids.

DAN. What's wrong with it?

JERRY. You wouldn't even sit out there.

DAN. She doesn't sit out there. She uses the key.

JERRY. It's not like her to be late.

DAN. She's putting the kids to bed. (DAN *picks up the photo of Joe.*)

JERRY. (*Crossing to desk phone.*) I'll call her mother's. If she hasn't left, I'll go pick her up. But if she has left, and she's not here, Irma will panic. And she's had enough to worry about today . . . (*He crosses back to windows and looks for* IRENE.)

DAN. Jerry. What was he like?

JERRY. Who?

DAN. Joe.

JERRY. He was her husband.

DAN. What was he like?

JERRY. He was a physicist at Columbia.

DAN. Into politics?

JERRY. (*Crossing to* DAN.) Joe? Hell, no. He was a genius. He was into light and sound and things that in the whole world, maybe a dozen other guys understood. Three of them Russian. At Columbia, they always thought, one day—a Nobel. You know what he was like? The son of a bitch was a saint.

DAN. No wonder it took two years.

JERRY. (*To himself.*) I think I'm going to leave my wife. I have to leave my wife. I'm leaving my wife.

DAN. (*Setting Joe's picture back on the sofa table.*) What?

JERRY. I am leaving my wife.

DAN. Since when?

JERRY. Tonight.

DAN. Are you sure you want to leave her?

JERRY. No. Yes. You were married.

DAN. Ten years.

JERRY. (*Sitting on sofa beside* DAN.) We're going on twelve. Divorced?

DAN. Yup.

JERRY. Kids?

DAN. No.

JERRY. I thought you were Catholic.

DAN. Lapsed.

JERRY. Guilty?

DAN. (*Rising and crossing to radiators.*) You're right. It is warm in here.

JERRY. Just tell me. How do you leave your wife?

DAN. You tell her.

JERRY. I know you tell her. What do you say?

DAN. 472-9044.

JERRY. That's what you say?

DAN. It's my lawyer's number.

JERRY. I wouldn't do that. You didn't do that. What happened?

DAN. (*Coming down to sofa.*) Same old story. I was getting deeper into politics. Trouble shooting for the party. A little trouble on the side. We lost touch.

JERRY. We *don't* touch.

DAN. It was the middle of the '74 campaign. I flew in from Ohio one night, walked in the front door, and the whole thing blew up.

JERRY. Is she all right? I mean, now?

DAN. She's fine.

JERRY. I'm responsible for Gloria.

DAN. Look, the day my wife became my ex-wife, she got married. She didn't have a wedding bouquet. She had the divorce papers in one hand and the marriage license in the other. It was an origami festival.

JERRY. Oh, my God . . .

DAN. What?

JERRY. Gloria will get married again. No. The old Gloria would get married again. The new Gloria will just move him in.

DAN. Maybe you shouldn't move out.

JERRY. I know he'll have a beard. What was yours like?

DAN. He was a football player.

JERRY. No kidding?

DAN. Herb Crowley.

JERRY. (*Rising; suddenly forgetting his own problems.*) "Crazy Feet" Crowley? You're kidding. He was one hell of a running back for the Giants. We traded him to Washington.

DAN. That's where I live. Washington.

JERRY. In '73. They really thought he'd make a difference. They gave up a first draft choice for him.

DAN. And two linemen.

JERRY. He never cut it with the Redskins. What happened to him?

DAN. My wife. She hit him on the blind side.

JERRY. I remember . . . when he started out, he was great.

DAN. It was a gradual deterioration. First the balance went. Then the peripheral vision. He started fumbling handoffs. By the end of the season, he couldn't find his feet. He retired.

JERRY. Jesus. She screwed him right out of the N.F.L. (*Trying to get his foot out of his mouth.*) I'm sorry. I didn't mean that. It's the heat.

DAN. (*Crossing to counter.*) You want some advice? Ride it out. Relax. Playing around isn't the disease. It's the symptom. Maybe it'll pass.

JERRY. How can it pass? There's someone else.

DAN. There's always someone else. Don't think about it.

JERRY. (*Taking off his sport jacket.*) I can't think about anything else. Except the temperature in this room. (JERRY *crosses to bar, takes a piece of ice, rubs his neck to cool off.*)

DAN. (*Bringing a bottle of bourbon to table and sitting.*) So, who is he?

JERRY. Who's who?

DAN. The guy.

JERRY. What guy?

DAN. With the beard. Gloria's guy.

JERRY. Gloria?

DAN. Your wife. Gloria.

JERRY. Gloria doesn't have a guy. (*Concerned; crossing to* DAN.) Who told you Gloria has a guy?

DAN. You said . . .

JERRY. I said?

DAN. You said there was someone else.

JERRY. There is.

DAN. So?

JERRY. Me. I've got someone else.

DAN. You? With the hot and cold flashes? Jerry, you devil, you.

JERRY. It's fantastic. Let me tell you, it's the last thing I ever expected. (*Sitting at the table.*) Look at me. I'm a whole new person. (JERRY *drops the ice in an ashtray, bends down suddenly and unties his shoelaces.*)

DAN. What are you doing?

JERRY. My laces are tight.

DAN. The commuter's paradise. An ignorant wife in the country and a loving mistress in the city. If you can afford it, you've got it made.

JERRY. I can't live that way.

DAN. She wants to get married. Right?

JERRY. We haven't talked about it.

DAN. Keep it that way.

JERRY. You don't understand. All your life, you dream about someone, and you think nothing can be as good as the dream. Then it happens, and its better.

DAN. Sometimes, you don't even dream . . . And then it happens, and it's better.

JERRY. Better than what?

DAN. Better than the dream you never had. (*Embarrassed.*) Hey, who talks about these things? Kids.

JERRY. My grandfather always said, "The kinder zolln reden when the heaner pischt."

DAN. What does that mean?

JERRY. Children should speak when chickens pee.

DAN. That's what that means?

JERRY. It loses something in translation.

DAN. So, where is this girl?

JERRY. In San Francisco.

DAN. Hell of a town, San Francisco. (*They both reflect.*) You haven't told Gloria, yet?

JERRY. Tonight. I tell her tonight.

DAN. Stay in town. Think about it.

JERRY. I could stay. No. Wednesday night I call my parents in Florida. (*Crossing to window; looking for* REENY.) I have to go home. Where is Reeny?

DAN. Who's the woman? Do I know her?

JERRY. Of course you know her.

DAN. Who is she?

JERRY. Irene.

DAN. Maybe you should call her mother's. Come on, who is she?

JERRY. Reeny.

DAN. I know. She's late.

JERRY. (*Crossing toward* DAN.) Reeny. Irene Porter. Reeny's the other woman.

DAN. Reeny?

JERRY. I am in love with Irene Porter. How else can I say it? (*With innocent pleasure.*) I am having an affair with Irene Porter. That's how I can say it.

DAN. (*Absorbing this.*) You're what?

JERRY. I shouldn't have said it.

DAN. Since when, you and Reeny?

JERRY. Since today.

DAN. (*Rising.*) But you said San Francisco.

JERRY. Right here. This room. This was the Fairmont Hotel. Out there, Alcatraz. She needed to get away.

DAN. (*Crossing to* JERRY.) Oh, she did, did she?

JERRY. Losing . . . The commercials . . . I told her about the commercials. And then we . . .

DAN. You what?

JERRY. It was very special. (DAN *punches* JERRY *very hard in the stomach.* JERRY *falls back onto the stairs.*)

DAN. It was fucking immoral!

JERRY. Yes, but I'm going to marry her. (*Reaching beneath himself, he finds a glass splinter.*) Glass!

(*He bends down and begins to search for more glass on the steps.* IRENE *enters the front door. She is the picture of efficiency—from the briefcase to the boots.*)

IRENE. Good. You're here.

DAN. (*Truly angry.*) You're late.

IRENE. (*Crossing to desk to deposit briefcase.*) Jerry, I'm here. You can stop cleaning. (IRENE *looks to coat hooks and hangs up coat.*)

DAN. Do you know what time it is?

JERRY. 10:13. I used the key. We were perfectly safe in the car. The doors were locked, but he said I should use the key.

DAN. You said nine o'clock.

IRENE. (*Crossing back to desk.*) I ran late. It was a busy day.

DAN. (*Sitting on edge of sofa table.*) It certainly was.

JERRY. I was worried about you.

IRENE. (*Sitting in armchair and taking off boots.*)
There are more important things to worry about. This
afternoon, I went to the office and sat down with
Jerry's books. Then I had a meeting with Ed Rios.

DAN. What happened to his returns last night?

IRENE. Human error. Like my campaign. After that,
I finally got to my mother's who insisted that I eat
something and listened to my daughter who knows I
won because everyone's parents in her class voted for
me. I then corrected my son's Social Science paper that
begins with Joan of Arc, concludes with his mother,
and is entitled "Important Losers of History." And
now I would like to get down to business. (IRENE *puts
her boots in the foyer; then crosses to desk and takes
two pamphlets from her briefcase.*)

DAN. What's on your mind?

IRENE. Money.

JERRY. We brought the contributors' cards.

IRENE. Last night I lost an election. Today I woke
up owing seventy-five thousand dollars for television
time.

JERRY. Give or take . . .

IRENE. Agreed?

DAN. Agreed.

IRENE. Gentlemen, if I were you, I would find myself
a capable attorney as soon as I reasonably could.

JERRY. Why?

IRENE. Because you are both a breath away from a
Federal indictment, a twenty-five thousand dollar fine
and a year in jail.

JERRY. (*To* DAN.) What is she talking about?

DAN. How the hell should I know?

IRENE. (*She hands first to* DAN *and then to* JERRY
two government pamphlets.) You may want to look
these over.

JERRY. What is this?

DAN. The Federal Election Campaign Act. With the amendments.

IRENE. (*Crossing to counter and fixing a drink.*) Title 18 is what you want.

JERRY. (*Crossing to sofa, sitting and looking at the pamphlet.*) Title 18 . . .

IRENE. Section 608.

JERRY. 608 . . .

IRENE. Limits on contributions and expenses.

DAN. The Supreme Court decision changes that section.

IRENE. Ah, hah. You've read it.

DAN. One of my *winning* candidates wrote it. What's the question?

JERRY. Why are we going to jail?

IRENE. (*Crossing Center.*) I do not owe seventy-five thousand dollars for television time. They are called "paid political announcements" because that's what they are—paid. In advance. By the Committee to Elect Irene Porter. Where did you get it? Where does it come from? Why is it owed? And who in the *hell* is the Committee to Elect Irene Porter?

DAN. (*To* JERRY.) You have a fine way of telling her everything.

JERRY. (*To* DAN.) My figures will stand up in any court. This was your part and you said it was legal.

DAN. (*Crossing to table.*) It is legal.

JERRY. (*To* IRENE.) He is the Committee to Elect Irene Porter.

IRENE. What?

JERRY. It's his money. He got it, and he spent it. For television time.

IRENE. One thousand dollars. Under the law, that's all you can spend. You know that.

Dan. I know what I can spend. What can you spend?

Irene. Every cent I have. It's my First Amendment Right.

Dan. You spent seventy-five thousand dollars. Under your First Amendment Right.

Irene. (*Crossing away from* Dan.) I have one checking account, one savings account, and one New York State Lottery Ticket. That's every cent I have, and it doesn't come close to seventy-five *hundred* dollars!

Dan. I loaned you seventy-five thousand dollars.

Irene. You did not.

Dan. Oh, yes, I did.

Irene. How could you loan it to me without my knowing about it?

Dan. Because if you knew about it, you wouldn't take it. We couldn't raise it, and I had to spend it.

Irene. Where did you get it? Where does it come from?

Dan. I got it. What difference does it make?

Irene. (*Crossing to desk telephone.*) My mother! You went to my mother! No wonder she won't let the children go, they're all she has left!

Dan. I did not go to your mother. I went to my bank. I borrowed the money in my name at my bank.

Irene. In your name?

Dan. In my name.

Irene. Against what?

Dan. The Connally Company.

Irene. Your business . . . ?

Dan. It's my name. It's my business.

Irene. You didn't. You couldn't. No campaign manager in his right mind puts up his own money for a candidate.

Dan. (*Too off-hand.*) It was an irrational act. You see, I wanted you to win. Forget it.

IRENE. Forget it? How can I forget it?

DAN. Because it's over. It's done.

JERRY. We're not going to jail anymore, right?

IRENE. How can I pay it back? I can't pay it back . . .

DAN. (*At window near table.*) Have I asked for it? Why do you think I had to be in Washington this morning?

JERRY. (*To* DAN.) Maybe you can write it off. We ought to look into that.

IRENE. (*To* JERRY.) He can't write it off. It's . . . (*Crossing to table; to* DAN.) Oh, my God. That's why you left at dawn.

DAN. I said goodbye.

IRENE. I didn't hear you.

DAN. I had to go.

JERRY. (*To himself.*) At dawn?

IRENE. You left. You didn't even leave a note.

DAN. We talked. I said, "How's your foot?" And you said, "I could run the mile." You said, "Have a good trip." And you rolled over.

JERRY. Rolled over?

IRENE. I didn't hear you.

JERRY. (*Rising.*) Just a minute, you two . . .

IRENE. (*To* DAN, *unaware of* JERRY.) They were good commercials. Even Ed Rios said they were good commercials.

DAN. They were great commercials. I came in too late. I couldn't make the right buys, and I didn't have enough money.

JERRY. The hell with the commercials.

DAN. (*To* IRENE.) I'd do it again.

IRENE. You wouldn't.

DAN. I couldn't.

IRENE. Oh, Dan . . .

JERRY. (*Crossing between* DAN *and* IRENE; *to* IRENE.) I have to talk to you.

DAN. (*To* IRENE.) I came back to tell you. But I couldn't tell you last night.

JERRY. (*To* DAN.) You came back last night?

IRENE. (*To* DAN.) Didn't you think I'd find out?

DAN. He was going to tell you. (To JERRY.) Why didn't you tell her?

JERRY. (*To* DAN.) What time did you come back last night?

DAN. She forgot to lock the door.

JERRY. (*To* IRENE.) Why don't you put up a sign? Welcome. Enter.

DAN. It was open.

JERRY. And you walked out this morning.

DAN. And locked it. You and your goddam key.

JERRY. (*Finally understanding.*) That's why you hit me.

IRENE. (*To* DAN.) You hit him?

JERRY. (*To* IRENE.) He didn't hurt me.

IRENE. (*Coming between* DAN *and* JERRY; *to* DAN.) Why did you hit him?

JERRY. (*To* IRENE; *it all makes sense now.*) You spent the night with him. You spent the afternoon with me.

IRENE. Jerry!

JERRY. That's why he hit me.

IRENE. (*To* DAN.) How could you hit him?

DAN. Because I didn't have a rope to strangle him.

JERRY. (*To* IRENE.) Because I told him . . .

IRENE. (*To* JERRY.) You told him?

JERRY. About us.

IRENE. How could you tell him?

JERRY. You were late.

IRENE. This is my home!

DAN. Oh, no. This was San Francisco.

IRENE. (*Crossing away from both men.*) This is the men's locker room!

JERRY. I was in love with you. I was going to leave my wife. Forget about me. Who am I? Best man. What about Joe? What about your husband? Think of him! (JERRY *takes Joe's picture and puts it in a more prominent position.*)

IRENE. He's dead.

JERRY. He would have won a Nobel. What about your children?

IRENE. They weren't home.

JERRY. They're my god-children.

IRENE. They were at my mother's!

JERRY. The people. You never gave a thought to the people.

IRENE. What people?

JERRY. They gave you their votes, their support!

IRENE. I LOST!

JERRY. They almost sent a nymphomaniac to Congress!

IRENE. (*Crossing to* DAN *at table; to* DAN.) HIT HIM!

JERRY. (*Fists up and ready to fight.*) Come on . . . Come on!

DAN. (*Sitting at table.*) Jerry, I'm not going to fight with you.

JERRY. No?

DAN. No!

JERRY. I win!

DAN. Jesus . . .

IRENE. (IRENE *leads* JERRY *to table and sits him down; she sits on arm of armchair.*) Jerry . . .

JERRY. (*To* IRENE.) I don't understand. I'm willing

to understand, but I don't understand. It's the women's movement, or something, isn't it? You're making a statement. Like Gloria when she keeps talking about her "sisters." She is an only child. I understand about equal work for equal pay. I'm for that, Irene. And I know the Supreme Court says it's your body. You control it.

IRENE. That's abortion.

JERRY. God forbid.

DAN. For once in your life, will you forget about being half responsible and half guilty?

JERRY. I can't. I'm half Jewish.

DAN. Jerry, listen to me. It's very simple. Face it, the woman was momentarily deranged. It's like combat fatigue. You never know how someone's going to react.

IRENE. (*She will deal with this as calmly as possible.*) One sexual experience is deranged?

DAN and JERRY. Two!

DAN. You have to admit you were under stress.

IRENE. Ah, that's right. Under stress, I, a perfectly conventional woman, turned into a sex maniac. That's what you're saying.

DAN. You had an emotional lapse. Under stress, the controls broke down.

IRENE. The dam burst?

DAN. (*Rising.*) Right. And that's the end of it.

IRENE. Moon madness. How about moon madness?

DAN. Call it anything you want.

IRENE. What do you call it when you bed down a parade of political groupies?

DAN. I call it *unimportant*, that's what I call it!

IRENE. (*Rising.*) For you, it's unimportant. For me, it's a nervous breakdown. If the shoe were on the other foot . . . If *he* (*Pointing to* JERRY.) had two women in twenty-four hours, what would you say to *him?*

DAN. Congratulations!

IRENE. (*Pausing, she walks away, then turns back to* DAN.) In my whole adult life, I have had one husband, two children, and two affairs . . .

DAN. What are you running for now? Sainthood?

IRENE. I thought you had some understanding. I thought you had some respect for me.

DAN. If you ever come back to your senses, I will respect the hell out of you.

IRENE. I am in full and complete possession of my senses. (To DAN.) You . . . Last night, I wanted and needed you . . . (To JERRY.) And today, Jerry, I thought you wanted and needed me. (*To both of them.*) And contrary to what your mothers may have taught you and your Puritan ethics and your childhood fairy tales, the sky did not fall. (*Pause.*) I liked it.

DAN. (*Angry; heading for the front door.*) The hell you did!

IRENE. I hated those commercials.

DAN. (*That stops him.*) What?

IRENE. I hated them. I hated the whole idea of them. I didn't want them. I never wanted them.

DAN. You just said they were great!

JERRY. No, you said they were great.

DAN. You stay out of this.

IRENE. (*To* DAN.) I didn't want your mass media, and I didn't want your money.

DAN. You thanked me. You were grateful. Who the hell did I do it for?

IRENE. Yourself! It was your campaign, your election. When I lost, you even made it your losing. You'll get every cent back.

DAN. You don't owe me a thing.

IRENE. I *won't* owe you a thing, and that's why I'm going to pay it back.

DAN. You haven't got it, you can't get it, and I won't take it!

IRENE. (*Really angry now.*) Oh, yes, you will! I was the token candidate. I was the picture on the poster. The idiot girl child who has to be patted and protected because she has mental lapses and the vapours.

DAN. I never said vapours.

IRENE. You implied vapours.

DAN. (*Nose-to-nose with* IRENE.) Look, you don't hear sex stories about Bella Abzug!

IRENE. Who knows what goes on under that hat?!

DAN. (*Crossing to table.*) There is no talking to you.

IRENE. Don't talk to me. Sweep it under the rug, because what you're really talking about is sin with a capital "S" and Eve and the Fall and, oh my God, Gloria is right. We are all sisters!

DAN. (*First to* JERRY; *then to* IRENE.) Oh, Mr. Dooley said it. He knew what we were in for. First we let 'em ride the bicycle, and then we give 'em the vote. It was the beginning of the end.

IRENE. It was the crossing of the Rubicon!

DAN. It *was* moon madness. And the vapours! You can call me when it passes! (DAN *storms out the front door, taking* JERRY's *coat instead of his own.*)

IRENE. (*Calling out the door after him.*) Equal rights! Not on your bus!

JERRY. (*Noticing the coat mix-up.*) Hey, wait a minute . . . Come back! (JERRY *crosses to door.*)

IRENE. (*Closing door.*) NO!

JERRY. He's got my coat!

IRENE. (*Crossing to counter for her drink.*) Jerry. Go home.

JERRY. (*Ingenuously.*) I can't. I can't go out without a coat.

IRENE. Jerry, please . . .

JERRY. I'm sorry. I apologize.

IRENE. For what?

JERRY. All of it. You see, you were everything to me. You were Eleanor Roosevelt. You were a perfect person.

IRENE. And what am I now?

JERRY. An *almost* perfect person.

IRENE. (*Toasting.*) I'll drink to that.

JERRY. Sit down, Reeny.

IRENE. (*Sitting at the table.*) I am very tired.

JERRY. I just want to ask you one question. How do you feel about New Jersey?

IRENE. New Jersey?

JERRY. Right across the bridge.

IRENE. (*Remembering.*) I have very warm feelings about—right across the bridge.

JERRY. (*Getting his briefcase from foyer and taking papers out.*) Good. It has to be New Jersey because of the tax situation and the girls. I'll have the girls weekends. I insist on that. From New Jersey, I cross the bridge. It's easy to get them. I can't live in the city. You wouldn't believe what walked down that block tonight. (JERRY *puts on his jacket and sits at the table.*)

IRENE. I walked down that block tonight.

JERRY. This afternoon, after we—you know—I did a lot of thinking and a lot of figuring. (*He has taken some papers out of his briefcase, and spreads them out on the table.*) Mortgage payments . . . Insurance . . . Real Estate taxes . . . I put my house in order.

IRENE. It always is.

JERRY. Look. Will you please just look?

IRENE. I want . . . a cup of tea.

JERRY. I've built up a hell of a good business. I mean, I don't stand around street corners shouting,

"Jerome T. Leeds, C.P.A., has done very well," flashing my tax shelters. But I can tell you. I have a loaf of bread under my arm.

IRENE. I'm glad.

JERRY. Gloria will get most of it. Twelve years. Three kids. How much are twelve years and three kids worth?

IRENE. (*Rising and crossing to sofa.*) Jerry, twelve years and three kids are worth everything.

JERRY. For the first few years you'll have to work.

IRENE. I need a vacation.

JERRY. That will have to wait.

IRENE. (*Lying down on sofa.*) Why should I work? I'm eligible for welfare.

JERRY. (*Rising.*) Irene, will you stop fooling around? Between Gloria and paying back Dan—we're not going to have that hanging over us—this whole thing is predicated on your supplemental income for at least three years.

IRENE. What whole thing?

JERRY. (*Crossing above* IRENE *and dropping a sheet of figures on her stomach.*) Our marriage.

IRENE. (*Sitting up.*) I can't marry you, Jerry.

JERRY. Irene, whatever you did, whatever you've done . . . No matter who, when, where or how many— I forgive you.

IRENE. I don't want to be forgiven.

JERRY. Don't apologize. Your past is dead.

IRENE. You can't do that!

JERRY. I've done it. It's done. You'll give up what's been, and I'll give up my home, my children, and a lot of bread.

IRENE. Jerry, you love your children.

JERRY. Weekends. I'll see them weekends. That's enough for children. (IRENE *tears* JERRY'S *papers into pieces.*) What are you doing?

IRENE. They're just figures, Jerry.

JERRY. It's because of my feelings that I'm making up figures. This afternoon . . .

IRENE. This afternoon it was San Francisco. Tonight, it's 84th Street. San Francisco was a trip we should have taken a long time ago. It was a beautiful trip, Jerry. I thank you.

JERRY. We can go anywhere.

IRENE. You want to go home.

JERRY. Will you marry me?

IRENE. No.

JERRY. Then, I'll go home. (*He takes torn papers from her and throws them away.*) We don't have to get married. Who gets married anymore? I'll stay in town two nights a week. (*He has packed up his briefcase. Putting on* DAN'S *coat and crossing down to* IRENE.) Not Wednesday. Wednesday I call my parents in Florida. We'll work it out. Irene, we are consenting adults.

IRENE. (*Rising.*) No, we're not. That's yes and a handshake and so long, fella, it's been swell. We grew up to be caring adults, Jerry. It must have been the neighborhood.

JERRY. I'm glad you lost. You know what I mean. If you hadn't lost, I wouldn't have had this afternoon. (*Buttoning the coat.*) There's a button missing.

IRENE. That's Dan's coat.

JERRY. (*Taking the coat off and handing it to* IRENE.) Reeny, the Mozart . . . That was Dan.

IRENE. (*Her oldest and dearest friend.*) I love you.

JERRY. I'll go home.

IRENE. And Jerry, when you get there, go upstairs and get into bed and roll over and touch her—and just take her on a trip.

JERRY. (*At front door.*) I'm not going back to San Francisco without you.

IRENE. Thank you.

JERRY. I'll take Gloria to Hawaii. (*He exits.*)

IRENE. (*Locks the door behind* JERRY, *begins to clean up the room, then suddenly crosses to the phone and dials it.*) Hello, Dan? (*Long pause as she listens to the message on* DAN'S *telephone answering machine.*) This is Irene Porter. I don't know what time it is. I waited for the beep. You took Jerry's coat with you. You left your coat here. It must have been moon madness, Mr. Dooley. (*She hangs up.*) I'll sew the button on. (*On second thought.*) The hell I will. (IRENE *hangs up the coat and switches out the room lights. She starts up the stairs, turning on the staircase lights. The door buzzer rings.*) Jerry, will you please go home. (*The buzzer rings again.*) Will you wait a minute? (*She opens the front door, and* DAN *lurches in. He is just this side of drunk.*)

DAN. Good. You have learned to lock the door. Now you must learn to say, "Who is it?" before you open the door.

IRENE. I just called you.

DAN. You called me?

IRENE. Welcome to the new world. My hand will not grow warts if I call you.

DAN. (*Turning on the room lights.*) I'm catching a cold.

IRENE. Where's Jerry's coat?

DAN. (*Crossing to sofa.*) I haven't got a coat. Why do you think I'm catching a cold?

IRENE. (*Straightening up the room.*) You took Jerry's coat. That's why I called you.

DAN. That's why I couldn't find it. It's at the Clover Bar. The Clover Bar is at Broadway and 83rd. With a tin ceiling. Like Dooley's out in Queens . . . what the hell . . . I came back to tell you . . . (IRENE *walks*

away from DAN.) No . . . the truth. This time that's
what you're going to get. I take full responsibility for
the last twenty-four hours. It was my fault. I take full
responsibility for the media and the money and the
last three weeks. It was my fault. But losing the election? You want the truth. That was your responsibility
and your fault!

IRENE. That's what you came back to tell me?

DAN. I was right. I knew it, and I proved it at the
Clover Bar. I have just completed an in-depth poll at
the Clover Bar. We got killed at the Clover Bar,
Reeny. (*He sits, heavily.*)

IRENE. That's yesterday's news, Dan. The election's
over. Why did you come back?

DAN. My coat . . .

IRENE. Dan.

DAN. You can't marry Jerry.

IRENE. He asked me. I let someone ask me. (*Sitting
in the armchair.*) He's married.

DAN. I was married.

IRENE. I know.

DAN. My divorce worked. My marriage didn't.

IRENE. Why not?

DAN. (*Genuinely puzzled.*) I don't know . . . (*He
starts the story.*) It was the middle of the '74 campaign. I flew in from Ohio one night, walked in the
front door . . . (*The truth.*) and found my wife in
bed with Herb Crowley.

IRENE. Herb Crowley?

DAN. "Crazy Feet" Crowley.

IRENE. An Indian?

DAN. A football player.

IRENE. What did you do?

DAN. I . . .

IRENE. I know. You hit him. Like you hit Jerry.

DAN. Yup. He beat the shit out of me.

IRENE. Well, you learned something.

DAN. I learned something. Always call first. I'm moving back to Washington tomorrow. That's what I came back to tell you.

IRENE. Last night it was the money. Tonight, it's Washington. You keep coming back to tell me what you're going to tell me but you never tell me.

DAN. You never let up, do you? Do you know why I waited three days to say "yes" to you?

IRENE. Because it's not like a marriage. You don't plunge in.

DAN. (*Rising; angrily; cutting her off.*) Because I knew you'd blow it and in politics winning is the only business. But I thought, what the hell, there's somebody left who still cares. A believer. I thought, times like these, why not? Your conscience. My smarts. It's a wrap! But oh, no, I should have known. You don't fool around with believers. They want too much. They want it all. You know why I threw good money after bad? Because I'm just as stubborn as you are. I wanted you to win so I could prove you were wrong. That the good guys don't win because they're good and deserving, but because the movers and the shakers, the guys like me, we make it happen. I wanted to shake you up, Reeny, shake some of that "greater good" out of your head. It didn't work. You're not going to change, and neither am I. You want commitment. Hell, you demand it and I can't marry you, Reeny! That's what I really came back to tell you.

IRENE. Last night, I couldn't think of anything worse than losing. There is something worse than losing . . . (*He thinks she will say, "Living without you".*) It is listening to you. Okay, I lost last night, but by God, I tried. Nothing changes in this world unless someone says, "I'll try!" Nothing happens . . .

DAN. (*Overlapping.*) My God, do you have to turn everything into a campaign speech?

IRENE. (*Rising.*) Why not? Maybe you got killed at the Clover Bar, but I didn't. I'm going to run again.

DAN. What?

IRENE. (*The statement has surprised herself; she considers it and approves.*) I'm going to run, and I am going to win. (*She exits into kitchen.*)

DAN. Why? Because trying is a virtue? Because caring is enough?

IRENE. (*Re-appearing with a tray, she puts it on the coffee table.*) You can't put down my conscience. I won't let you. I'm scared. But so is everyone else. I learned something out there . . . in the ring, in the real world, with the big boys. I'm good. That's right. I'm as good as any of them and better than most. I am knowledgeable. I am effective. And when I win, I know I can deliver. (*She puts a dirty ashtray on tray and crosses to table.*)

DAN. You are flat out. You are broke. And you are crazy. Will you ever, once in your life, be practical?

IRENE. Practical? Tell me about practical. Tell me about seventy-five thousand dollars worth of practical.

DAN. (*Picking up tray, he crosses to her.*) I explained all that.

IRENE. (*Putting glasses, ashtrays and bottles from table onto tray.*) You don't explain. You rationalize. But you put up the money—for me. Well, this time I am going to raise the money. I am going to use your media. I am going to do it all. (*She crosses to the counter.*)

DAN. (*Following with tray.*) My God, you have heard something. Maybe you even learned something.

IRENE. (*Putting ice bucket and whiskey bottles on tray.*) They're going to walk into that booth, close that curtain and *buy* me.

DAN. Who knows? Maybe you'll pull it off. Morton Davis has got to retire sometime. Two years . . . Maybe you'll get to Washington. (*He carries tray into kitchen.*)

IRENE. (*Caught up in her new political fervor.*) Washington? (*Pause.*) I don't care about Washington. They don't care about us. Why should they? It has to start here. And if I have to shake six million hands to do it . . . (*She turns off the light switch for the chandelier above the table.*) then I will shake six million hands.

DAN. (*Turns off kitchen light.*) Six million? What the hell are you running for? (*He turns off the counter lamp.*)

IRENE. Mayor.

DAN. Mayor?

IRENE. Mayor of New York City. (*She turns off the sofa lamp.*)

DAN. I know Gracie Mansion's a nice house. You'd have a yard for the kids. But it's impossible. To begin with, there's the primary . . .

IRENE. (*Clearing her desk for action.*) I win primaries.

DAN. In one district. There **are** *twenty*-one key districts.

IRENE. I've got a base. I've **got a** damned good political base. I've got Porelli.

DAN. (*He's interested.*) Porelli's Manhattan. What about Brooklyn?

IRENE. In Brooklyn, there's Smith. He loves me. (*She turns out the desk lamp.*)

DAN. (*Crossing to front door.*) There's Staten Island, the Bronx, Queens . . .

IRENE. (*Gathering up boxes of contributors' cards.*) You were raised in Queens.

DAN. *If* you could get . . . (*He locks the front door.*) the unions, the regulars, the fat cats . . .

IRENE. The people!

DAN. The money, first. Then the media. Then the votes. And *then* the people. That's the drill. (*He switches off the foyer light.*) Will you ever get that into your head? (*He crosses past* IRENE *and begins to climb the stairs.*)

IRENE. Dan, do you know what we're doing?

DAN. I know exactly what we're doing. We are planning a winning campaign.

IRENE. (*Following him up the stairs.*) Dan, let me re-phrase the question . . . (IRENE *exits up the stairs, as . . .*)

THE CURTAIN FALLS

APPENDIX

Sound over Television P. 20, 21—Ed Rios' Voice

In Queens, Benjamin Rosenthal returns to Congress for his eighth term. In the ninth Congressional District, it is James Delaney, the winner, his sixteenth term. In the Bronx, an easy victory for Mario Biaggi on the Democratic and Republican lines. And in Brooklyn, Shirley Chisholm has no trouble retaining her seat. Charles Rangle has a clean sweep in the nineteenth, and in Manhattan, in the forty-first, it is now, Irene Porter the winner over incumbent Morton Davis.

(Pause.)

In the sixth Congressional District, Lester Wolff is the winner. In the fourteenth, Frederick Richmond returns to Congress. In the sixteenth, as expected, it is an easy win for Elizabeth Holtzman. In the eighteenth, it is Howard Koch, winning handily. Theodore Weiss is the winner in the twentieth. In the seventeenth, it is John Murphy the winner, and in the eleventh, James Scheuer returns to Congress. In the third, fourth and fifth Districts in Long Island, all incumbents were re-elected, John Wydler beating Allard Lowenstein, Norman Lent defeating Gerald Halpern and James Ambro the winner over Howard T. Hogan, Jr. In Westchester, Richard Ottinger retains his seat and in the twenty-fifth it is Hamilton Fish, Jr. over Minna Peyser. And in the twenty-second, Jonathan Bingham returns to the House.

We will now go to the boards of the Senate races around the country. In Maine, it is Senator Edmund

Muskie returning with fifty-seven percent of the vote. In Massachusetts, the Kennedy magic is still effective. Edward Kennedy with seventy-one percent of the vote. Turning to New Jersey, it is Harrison Williams with sixty-two percent. In New York, Daniel Moynihan defeats James Buckley with fifty-two percent, and Lowell Weicker will continue to represent Connecticut with over fifty-eight percent of the vote. In Pennsylvania, that catsup money paid off for H. J. Heinz, and in Rhode Island it is John Chafee with over fifty-eight percent. In California, S. I. Hayakawa gave a knock-out blow to Democrat John Tunney. William Proxmire returns to the Senate with over one million votes.

PROPERTY LIST

ACT ONE—Pre-Set Onstage

On Dining Table:

1 ashtray (full)
1 deli tray
2 chicken buckets
2 pizza boxes
10 dirty plates
1 clean plate with 2 green olives on UR corner of table
25 clean wine glasses
CHECK: DL corner of table clear
1 bottle bourbon (Jack Daniels)
4 clean plastic tumblers

On Buffet:

1 empty wine bottle
4 dirty plates
2 dirty wine glasses

On Desk:

1 ashtray (full)
1 chicken bucket
3 dirty plates
1 telephone
1 wastebasket (DS)
1 desk blotter
1 typewriter

1 accordion file
1 cup with pens and pencils
1 dictionary
1 appointment book
3 telephone books
2 posters
1 First Aid kit (left drawer)

On Counter:

LITTLE COUNTRY THEATRE

1 bottle scotch
1 ice bucket with ice
1 lighter
1 box Kleenex
1 chicken bucket
1 pizza box
5 dirty plates
4 dirty glasses
6 clean on-the-rocks glasses
1 empty wine bottle

On Sofa Table:

1 deli tray
1 empty wine bottle
15 clean wine glasses
2 posters

On Sofa:

1 kid's sweater or jacket

On Coffee Table:

1 ashtray (full)
6 party noise-makers
6 dirty plates

1 stack cocktail napkins
5 dirty wine glasses

On Left End Table:

3 dirty plates
3 noise-makers

On Right End Table:

1 picture of "Joe"
2 campaign hats

On Right Armchair:

1 campaign hat

On Left Armchair:

1 afghan
CHECK: On Act 1, Scene 1 spikes

On Left Armchair End Table:

1 telephone
1 ashtray (full)
2 dirty paper plates

At TV:

4 extra chairs
CHECK: Power ON
       Volume OFF
       On Act 1, Scene 1 spikes

At Coat-Tree:

1 baseball bat
1 baseball

1 pair rollerskates
1 football helmet
1 pair football shoulderpads
assorted children's clothing
CHECK: (2) hooks free

On Foyer Table:

1 children's box game
1 campaign hat
2 dirty plates

On Stairs:

4 dirty plates
2 pizza boxes
3 campaign hats
2 posters

On Bookcase:

1 banner

In Umbrella Stand:

1 hockey stick
1 baton
assorted sports equipment

ACT ONE—Pre-Set Offstage

In Kitchen:

1 rigged bottle of champagne filled with gingerale
2 break-away champagne glasses
1 tray with
　2 mugs with very little tea
　　1 tea with milk

2 plates of Russian cake
2 forks
2 spoons
1 sugar bowl
1 creamer
1 pot of lukewarm tea
1 dustpan with whiskbroom
1 metal wastebasket
1 pot of flowers
1 mom-cat poster on door
1 empty glass
CHECK: door open
1 kitchen towel

PERSONAL PROPERTIES

IRENE (Colleen Dewhurst)

  1 keychain with key to fit front door
  1 briefcase with
    1 legal pad
    3 copies of Campaign Finance Laws

DAN (George Hearn)

  1 pack of Camel regulars
  1 box matches
  1 fresh *N.Y. Times* per perf.
  1 fresh *N.Y. Daily News* per perf.

JERRY (Rex Robbins)

  1 keychain with key to fit front door
  1 briefcase with
    1 accountant's ledger
    1 stack of bills
    3 ballpoint pens
    1 desk calendar
    2 stapled financial statements

Scene Break between Act 1, Scene 1 and Act 1, Scene 2

STRIKE: All trash from party to leave the following working props. Also leave all dressing which was not set specifically for Act 1, Scene 1.

LEAVE:

On Dining Table:

    1 ashtray (clean)
    1 box Kleenex
    1 centerpiece

On Counter:

    1 bottle bourbon
    1 bottle scotch
    1 ice bucket
    1 lighter
    4 clean glasses
    (Strike water pitcher to kitchen)

On Desk:

    1 ashtray (clean)
    1 telephone
    1 wastebasket

On Coffee Table:

    1 ashtray (clean)

On Sofa Table:
    1 lamp (permanent)

On Right End Table:

    1 picture of "Joe"

On Left Armchair:

    1 afghan
    CHECK: on Act 1, Scene 2 spikes

On Left Armchair End Table:

    1 *N.Y. Times* folded

1 telephone
1 ashtray (clean)

At TV:

CHECK: on Act 1, Scene 2 spikes

Scene Break between Act 1, Scene 1 and Act 1, Scene 2

On Coat-Tree:

1 briefcase (Jerry)
1 raincoat (Jerry)
assorted children's clothes
STRIKE: Dan's raincoat to dressing room

At Stairs:

CHECK: small pieces of glass cleaned
         large pieces of glass on steps

On Bookcase:

1 banner

SET: You have set the following during the Scene Break:

Jerry's briefcase
Jerry's coat
moved the TV
moved the water pitcher
newspaper

During Intermission

STRIKE: Jerry's briefcase to dressing room
        Jerry's coat to dressing room
        tray
        2 mugs
        banner
        ice from ice bucket

SET: fill whiskey bottles
     4 clean glasses on bar counter
     pitcher of ice in kitchen
     bowl of fruit on dining room table
     decorative bowl on sofa table

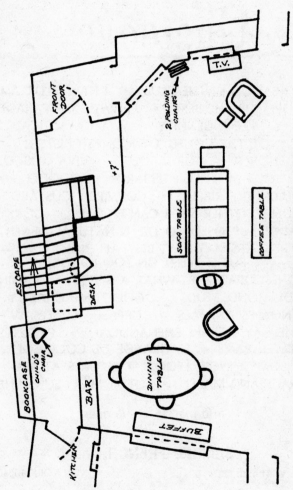

Scene Design "AN ALMOST PERFECT PERSON"

Musicals...

CHICAGO • THE CLUB • I HAVE A DREAM
HOPE FOR THE BEST • PRIVATES ON PARADE
YANKEE INGENUITY • VIA GALACTICA
"NOT *THE* COUNT OF MONTE CRISTO?!"
PUSHOVER • TURNABOUT • VIVA MEXICO!
OLD MOTHER HUBBARD • ODODO
JACK THE RIPPER • COWARDY CUSTARD
DON'T BOTHER ME, I CAN'T COPE • GORKY
AIN'T SUPPOSED TO DIE A NATURAL DEATH
"PROGRESS MAY HAVE BEEN ALL RIGHT ONCE—
BUT IT WENT ON TOO LONG"
IONESCOPADE • WHAT A SPOT! • RAISIN
DIAMOND STUDS • GOODTIME CHARLEY
NOAH'S ANIMALS • GREASE • SEESAW
THE GAY LIFE • SHENANDOAH • PRETZELS
PETER PAN • EL GRANDE DE COCA-COLA
SOMETHING'S AFOOT • DAMES AT SEA
MACK AND MABEL • LITTLE MARY SUNSHINE

Information on Request

SAMUEL FRENCH, Inc.

25 West 45th St.   NEW YORK 10036

6 RMS RIV VU
BOB RANDALL
(Little Theatre) Comedy
4 Men, 4 Women, Interior

A vacant apartment with a river view is open for inspection by prospective tenants, and among them are a man and a woman who have never met before. They are the last to leave and, when they get ready to depart, they find that the door is locked and they are shut in. Since they are attractive young people, they find each other interesting and the fact that both are happily married adds to their delight of mutual, yet obviously separate interests.

> ". . . a Broadway comedy of fun and class, as cheerful as a rising souffle. A sprightly, happy comedy of charm and humor. Two people playing out a very vital game of love, an attractive fantasy with a precious tincture of truth to it."—*N.Y. Times.*
> ". . . perfectly charming entertainment, sexy, romantic and funny."—*Women's Wear Daily.*

Royalty, $50—$35

WHO KILLED SANTA CLAUS?
TERENCE FEELY
(All Groups) Thriller
6 Men, 2 Women, Interior

Barbara Love is a popular television 'auntie'. It is Christmas, and a number of men connected with her are coming to a party. Her secretary, Connie, is also there. Before they arrive she is threatened by a disguised voice on her Ansaphone, and is sent a grotesque 'murdered' doll in a coffin, wearing a dress resembling one of her own. She calls the police, and a handsome detective arrives. Shortly afterwards her guests follow. It becomes apparent that one of those guests is planning to kill her. Or is it the strange young man who turns up unexpectedly, claiming to belong to the publicity department, but unknown to any of the others?

> ". . . is a thriller with heaps of suspense, surprises, and nattily cleaver turns and twists . . . Mr. Feeley is technically highly skilled in the artificial range of operations, and his dialogue is brilliantly effective."—The Stage. London.

Royalty, $50—$25

THE SEA HORSE

EDWARD J. MOORE

(Little Theatre) Drama
1 Man, 1 Woman, Interior

It is a play that is, by turns, tender, ribald, funny and suspenseful. Audiences everywhere will take it to their hearts because it is touched with humanity and illuminates with glowing sympathy the complexities of a man-woman relationship. Set in a West Coast waterfront bar, the play is about Harry Bales, a seaman, who, when on shore leave, usually heads for "The Sea Horse," the bar run by Gertrude Blum, the heavy, unsentimental proprietor. Their relationship is purely physical and, as the play begins, they have never confided their private yearnings to each other. But this time Harry has returned with a dream: to buy a charter fishing boat and to have a son by Gertrude. She, in her turn, has made her life one of hard work, by day, and nocturnal love-making; she has encased her heart behind a facade of toughness, utterly devoid of sentimentality, because of a failed marriage. Irwin's play consists in the ritual of "dance" courtship by Harry of Gertrude, as these two outwardly abrasive characters fight, make up, fight again, spin dreams, deflate them, make love and reveal their long locked-up secrets.

"A burst of brilliance!"—*N.Y. Post.* "I was touched close to tears!"—*Village Voice.* "A must! An incredible love story. A beautiful play?"—*Newhouse Newspapers.* "A major new playwright!"—*Variety.*

ROYALTY, $50-$35

THE AU PAIR MAN

HUGH LEONARD

(Little Theatre) Comedy
1 Man, 1 Woman, Interior

The play concerns a rough Irish bill collector named Hartigan, who becomes a love slave and companion to an English lady named Elizabeth, who lives in a cluttered London town house, which looks more like a museum for a British Empire on which the sun has long set. Even the door bell chimes out the national anthem. Hartigan is immediately conscripted into her service in return for which she agrees to teach him how to be a gentleman rather after the fashion of a reverse Pygmalion. The play is a wild one, and is really the never-ending battle between England and Ireland. Produced to critical acclaim at Lincoln Center's Vivian Beaumont Theatre.

ROYALTY, $50-$35